VIKING
BANNER ADVERTISING

Viking Banner Advertising Page

Chapter 1:

An Introduction to Banner Ads

Banner advertising has come a long way since its humble beginnings centuries ago. Yes, that's right... centuries ;)

Flip through any old newspaper or publication from the American colonial era and you'll find rectangular banner ads pitching everything from beer to stockings, complete with a main image, carefully chosen brand colors, a motto or unique selling proposition, and even a call-to-action!

Of course, we're not here to discuss old print banner ads for stylish powdered wigs or state-of-the-art wooden dentures (although it is useful to remember how long the ancestors of today's digital banners have been around). In this guide we're going to discuss modern digital banner ads in all their glory. So, for starters, what are they?

What are banner Ads?

Basically, banner advertisements are actionable, clickable, tappable images that invite web visitors to buy, learn about, or receive something in exchange for a click-through. These ads can appear anywhere and are typically seen within and around the content of various websites such as the header area on a forum page, the sidebar of a blog or news site, or even squeezed in among the paragraphs of a news article.

These banner ads come in all shapes and sizes (typically variations of the trusty old rectangle) and will either be static (.jpg, .png, or .gif) images or animated (.gif or Flash) banners. In more recent years, some businesses have been leveraging "Rich Media" banner ads that do all sorts of whacky stuff like send a car zooming across your screen in front of the article you were reading. And these ads aren't going anywhere soon. Banner ads still make up around 34% of all online ad spending, second only to Search Engine Marketing (SEM).

So, since they've been around for hundreds of years and businesses are spending a ton on them every year, clearly they work. The question is, should you be using them in your business?

Chapter 2:
Why You Should
Be Using Them

There are a host of reasons you would/should use banner ads in your business. We'll cover several of them here:

What Are Your Goals?

The general goal of banner ads is to take a visitor, who clicks on one of them, through to one of your web properties. But beyond this you may have more specific goals. This could include bringing them directly to a sales or product page in hopes of them making a purchase. Or perhaps you're simply doing a list building campaign and trying to gain leads or contact info by forwarding them to a landing page with a free offer or gift. Maybe your goal is to learn more about your market, in which case you might be sending them to a survey or questionnaire.

The final goal for click-throughs that we'll mention is simply content marketing. Perhaps you're simply trying to get your blog posts and articles in front of a lot of visitors in order to build a following, provide useful information, and perhaps even make a "soft pitch" within this content. Another sub-goal of content marketing worth mentioning is building a retargeting audience. There's plenty of data justifying this approach. People who are retargeted via banner ads are 70% more likely to convert! So the idea here is to simply stick a retargeting pixel on your site when you send visitors to your content (check out our retargeting guide for more detailed info on this). You can then retarget them wherever they are on the web with more relevant banner ads now that they are familiar with you and this time you can aim for something more desirable like a sale or an opt-in.

Other Benefits

One very useful but less talked about benefit of banner advertising is brand awareness. You've seen this work a thousand times. Year 'round you might see tv commercials for "Smiley Taxi Cabs". It's not like you're sitting in your living room and suddenly bolt upright and call a cab at that moment. You don't need one. But weeks or maybe months later when you're leaving a birthday party after having a bit to drink and you need a cab, who are you going to google on your smartphone? Yup. Smiley Cab. The same goes for banner ads. Even when people don't click on them, you'll be subtly building top-of-mind awareness for your business and expanding the visual familiarity of your brand.

Another benefit of banner advertising is the ability to track, assess, and test effectiveness. There are several metrics that can be used to measure various levels of effectiveness. The most basic level of assessment is your Click-through Rate or CTR. You can gauge the financial success of your ads by comparing your CTR against your advertising expenses which gives you your cost per click or CPC. Beyond this you can actually track the results of click-throughs (sales or opt-ins) versus your ad expenses. This can give you your cost per lead and cost per sale. Using conversion pixels you can test for even more complex results such as how far visitors get into your funnel or which blog posts they read after landing on your site.

So that's the "why" of banner advertising. Let's talk about the "where"...

Chapter 3:
Where to Conduct Banner Advertising

Know Your Target Market

Where you place your banner ads is mostly based on your goals and target market. So logically your first step should be to know and learn as much as you can about your target market. Understand your buyer personality, behavior and motives. Research your audience using existing studies or data. Look for case studies that reveal what has worked in the past for your niche. Or you can even do your own research by analyzing past advertising and sales data from your own records or by conducting surveys and polls on your target market. Also, just be aware of what people are saying and expressing by taking time to regularly monitor social media groups and forums in your target market.

Establish Your Goals

Looking at the goals mentioned in the previous section, you need to have a clear goal set for each banner ad campaign you run. Are you testing the waters for a new product idea? Then maybe your goal this time is to get visitors to a survey to gauge interest in the idea as well as to build an "early bird" list of leads to sell to when the product is finished. Maybe your goal is straight forward sales. Whatever it is, you'll need to know before you start planning where to display your banner ads.

Where to Display

Once you've got your target audience and goals sorted out, it's time to pick where to stick those ads. One option is to manually choose display locations. You can do this by reaching out to website owners, forums, and blogs in your niche. If you're selling an internet marketing tool, go pay for a banner placement in the header area of the Warrior Forum. If you're promoting your new book, find a popular blog for books in your genre and approach the owner about sidebar ads.

When using this manual method, be sure to research the metrics of the given site, blog, or forum. Naturally you'll want to display your ad in places with a reasonable level of traffic and a positive reputation to ensure your advertising dollars are spent well. You can learn a lot about websites by researching them on Alexa.

The manual method we've just described can be very effective but it can also be time-consuming and difficult. Many marketers prefer to do general targeting via a major ad network. Probably the most popular example of this would be the Google Adwords Network. Here, you'll simply make some targeting/audience and/or keyword decisions within your Google Adwords creation process (check out our Google Adwords guide for more info) and provide the right banner images (discussed below). Google Adwords will then begin showing your banner ads in the locations that it's data determines are best for your desired audience.

Another great option is to use a retargeting platform with multi-network reach like AdRoll. This means you install retargeting pixels on your site and build a retargeting audience which you can then follow around the web with your banner ads via several different networks/exchanges including Facebook and Google Adwords. In these cases, the retargeting platform generally does all the hard work for you.

Chapter 4: Designing Your Banner Ad

Tools

There are several tools you can use to create a banner ad. If you've got design skills, you can use any graphic design program like Adobe Photoshop or Gimp. However, many businesses prefer a super quick solution specifically designed for non-designers to create banner ads, such as BannerSnack.

Shape, Size, and Format

You'll need to make sure you have a variety of banner ad sizes available for use in your campaigns. You can get your ad sizes from the IAB (Interactive Advertising Bureau) or simply follow the recommendations of the ad network you're using. For example, Google AdWords recommends 300 x 250, 336 x 280, 728 x 90, 300 x 600, and 320 x 100 versions of your ads. Again, a banner ad solution like BannerSnack can make this process super easy.

Another important detail is going to be format. If you're going to use static images, you'll want to use .jpeg, .jpg, .png, and .gif file formats. If you're trying to do animated banners, you'll be dealing with .swf and .gif files. It's also important to consider the file size. This depends on your ad network. For example, Google's display network requires files to be 150KB or smaller.

Design Ideas

If you are indeed using a solution like BannerSnack, the best option for design and style is to use a template and stick with it's general layout. However, here are some general best practices to consider.

Be mindful of your brand or product colors and try to focus on just two or three primary or secondary colors for your ad. Use high quality images that are appealing and grab the attention of your audience (incorporate the things you learned while researching your audience). Ensure you properly use contrasting colors to make your text and CTA buttons pop out. For example, it would be silly to put white button text on a yellow button on a light orange background. A lot of this is common sense. If it doesn't pop out for you, it probably won't pop out for your audience. Also, be sure to balance main ideas and empty space. Jamming too much imagery and text into a banner can be counter productive.

Test, Test, and Test Again

Your goal within the ad campaign is to maximize the effectiveness of each dollar you spend. So it's a good idea to create several variations of your banner ads and review the results to see which ones perform best. You might try different CTA phrases like "learn more", "join now" and "add to cart". See if one background image grabs more clicks than another. Heck, see if maybe a red button beats a blue one. The point is, you want to squeeze as much value as you can from your advertising dollar so test several variations and see what gives you the lowest CPC.

Battle Plan

In conclusion, there's plenty of evidence that banner ads work great depending on your business, audience, and goals. So follow these steps below and get started right now:

Step 1: Learn everything you can about your target audience.

Step 2: Establish your banner ad goals.

Step 3: Determine which ad network or specific websites meet your needs.

Step 4: Using the size/shape guidelines of your chosen ad network or locations, design your banner images using the ideas discussed above.

Step 5: Test several variants and try to find a winner or two that will bring you the best CPC and ROI.

Don't put this off till later. Execute these steps today!